THIS NOTEBOOK BELONGS TO:

____

Made in United States
Orlando, FL
03 March 2023

30640985R00070